TAKE A MINUTE 01
FOR THE SELF-EVALUATION TEST

As a responsible person, I
take good care of my friends
and family.   Yes ☐   No ☐

I take good care of my
business and the people I
work with.   Yes ☐   No ☐

I take as much time to care
for MYSELF as I do for
family, friends, and
business.   Yes ☐   No ☐

I take time every day to do
things for myself that will
improve my outlook, my
attitude, and MYSELF.   Yes ☐   No ☐

My good attitude and
feelings about myself help
me deal positively with
others in business, at home,
and with MYSELF!   Yes ☐   No ☐

**IF YOU HAVE ANSWERED *NO* TO
EVEN ONE OF THESE QUESTIONS,
YOU NEED TO READ**

Other Books by Spencer Johnson, M.D.

WHO MOVED MY CHEESE?
An Amazing Way to Deal with Change

THE ONE MINUTE MANAGER®
Increase Productivity, Profits, and Your Own Prosperity
(coauthored with Kenneth Blanchard, Ph.D.)

THE ONE MINUTE MOTHER™
The Quickest Way for You to Help Your Children Learn to
Like Themselves and Want to Behave Themselves

THE ONE MINUTE FATHER™
The Quickest Way for You to Help Your Children Learn to
Like Themselves and Want to Behave Themselves

THE ONE MINUTE $ALES PERSON
The Quickest Way to More Sales with Less Stress
(coauthored with Larry Wilson)

THE ONE MINUTE TEACHER™
How to Teach Others to Teach Themselves
(coauthored with Constance Johnson, M.Ed.)

THE PRECIOUS PRESENT
The Gift That Makes You Happy Whenever You Choose

YES OR NO: *The Guide to Better Decisions*

THE VALUETALE™ SERIES *for children:*

THE VALUE OF BELIEVING IN YOURSELF, The Story of Louis Pasteur

THE VALUE OF COURAGE, The Story of Jackie Robinson

THE VALUE OF CURIOSITY, The Story of Christopher Columbus

THE VALUE OF DEDICATION, The Story of Albert Schweitzer

THE VALUE OF FANTASY, The Story of Hans Christian Andersen

THE VALUE OF HONESTY, The Story of Confucius

THE VALUE OF HUMOR, The Story of Will Rogers

THE VALUE OF IMAGINATION, The Story of Charles Dickens

THE VALUE OF KINDNESS, The Story of Elizabeth Fry

THE VALUE OF PATIENCE, The Story of the Wright Brothers

THE VALUE OF SAVING, The Story of Ben Franklin

THE VALUE OF SHARING, The Story of the Mayo Brothers

THE VALUE OF UNDERSTANDING, The Story of Margaret Mead

For Lauren

Spencer Johnson

2005

'01 One Minute For Yourself™

Previously published as
One Minute For Myself™

Spencer Johnson, M.D.

QUILL
William Morrow
New York

Dedicated to
my best friend

It is the policy of William Morrow and Company, and its imprints
and affiliates, recognizing the importance of preserving what has
been written, to print the books we publish on acid-free paper, and
we exert our best efforts to that end.

Library of Congress Cataloging-in-Publication Data

Johnson, Spencer.
    [One minute for myself]
    One minute for yourself / Spencer Johnson.
        p.   cm.
    Originally published: One minute for myself. New York :
W. Morrow, c1985.
    ISBN 0-688-16356-4 (alk. paper)
    1. Happiness.   2. Self-esteem.   3. Interpersonal relations.
I. Title.
BF575.H27J65   1998
158—dc21   -   98-35603
                                                          CIP

Printed in the United States of America

First Quill Edition 1998

20 19 18 17 16 15

www.williammorrow.com

Contents

Acknowledgments

Many people have helped me over the years to see that taking better care of yourself helps you *and* others.

I would like to publicly praise a few of them:

Kenneth Blanchard, Ph.D., my coauthor of *The One Minute Manager* and my good friend, for what he taught me—by example—about keeping a sense of humor and having a good attitude.

Herbert Benson, M.D., for what he taught me about reducing stress through relaxation.

Harold Bloomfield, M.D., for what he taught me about being my own best counselor.

Norman Cousins for what he taught me about laughing and changing my personal perspective.

Sharon Huffman for what she taught me about creating beauty and having a Master Plan.

Gerald Jampolsky, M.D., for what he taught me about finding love by letting go of fear.

My agent, Margret McBride, and the Margret McBride Literary Agency, for all their help.

All of the people who helped at William Morrow and Company, especially Larry Hughes, for their faith in me and their belief in what I do.

Gerald Nelson, M.D., the originator of *The One Minute Scolding*, for what he taught me about discipline and the difference between behavior and worth.

Carl Rogers, Ph.D., for what he taught me about creating peace within myself and with other people.

And especially my sons for what they continue to teach me about caring.

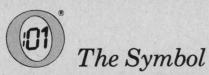 *The Symbol*

The One Minute symbol—a one-minute readout from the face of a modern watch—is intended to remind each of us to take one minute to stop, look, and see how we can take good care of ourselves—as well and as often—as we take care of others.

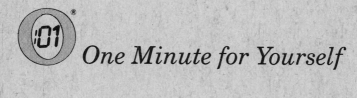

One Minute for Yourself

ONCE there was a businessman who was looking for greater personal success.

He wanted to be happier—at work and at home. He wanted more balance in his life.

While some people thought he was beginning to do well, the man knew that something essential was missing in his life.

Often he pushed aside this disquieting feeling. He told himself he was doing fine. But he knew he was working too hard and too long for his success.

When he took the courage to look, he saw that his relationships—both business and personal—lacked something.

And when he was alone, he did not always like the relationship he had with himself.

At times, the man wondered if it was too much to hope for: both success in his work and a personal inner peace.

He thought it must be a rare person, indeed, who was fortunate enough to have the best of both worlds.

None-the-less, the man hoped that someday he would meet such an individual—someone who not only knew the answer and lived it, but who would also share the secret with him.

"Perhaps," he thought, "such a secret is too personal to share with a stranger. If I only knew someone . . ."

Then he remembered someone who had become more successful in his work, and happier in his life.

"Uncle," as everyone in the family called him, seemed to enjoy everything, from good health to great wealth—though the man had heard it wasn't always that way.

Uncle also appeared to enjoy a happy family and social life. He always looked happy, as did other people when they were around him. He remembered how happy *he* felt when he was with his uncle.

Uncle seemed to know how to make both himself and other people happy.

He wondered why he hadn't spoken more in depth with his uncle before. It had always been just light conversation at family gatherings.

He telephoned and asked to see him. They arranged to meet the next day.

H<small>E</small> felt his uncle's warmth as he entered the older man's home. As soon as he was comfortable, he ventured, "Uncle, may I ask you why you are so successful—at work and in life?"

Uncle smiled and said, "Do you mean inner success or outer success?"

The younger man admitted, "I'm not sure."

"That's a good beginning," Uncle said, "not being sure. It means you're more receptive to something new. As we talk, you may be surprised that most of our conversation will be about *inner* success.

"I hope," Uncle encouraged, "you'll see that your finding inner success is the best, easiest, and in fact, the *only* way to achieve and enjoy everything else in life."

The man was already beginning to feel he had come to talk with the right person.

Uncle admitted, "When I wasn't happy with myself, I had to work longer to succeed and I didn't fully enjoy my success. And I was harder on the people around me.

"In fact, I didn't have much time for the more important parts of my life, including my wife, family, friends and colleagues."

Uncle admitted. "I used to be a workaholic."

The younger man asked, "What changed?"

"*I* did," Uncle answered. "I learned how to take better care of myself and to show the people around me how to take better care of themselves.

"Workaholics," Uncle said, "think they are happy. That's because they kid themselves. Workaholics, in fact, lose themselves in their work so that they never have to look at themselves.

"Other people do this by filling their life with activities. They confuse activity with productivity.

"The deception is they think they are accomplishing a lot because they are busy. In reality, they never deal with what's important.

"I now do first things first," Uncle said. "Before I can manage my life, I need to manage myself."

The nephew said, "So you are really saying that the better you manage your inner self, the more you enjoy all that life has to offer."

Uncle leaned forward and said, "That's a *truth*.

"Not only do you experience more outer success, but inside you feel balanced and peaceful."

The skeptical man said, "It sounds too simple to me and too good to be true."

His uncle said, "I don't blame you for doubting. But the truth is that the secret is so practical and powerful, that when you do it, everyone wins— you, others and ultimately the whole world."

As if to make the secret very clear, the older man wrote something on a piece of paper, passed it to his nephew and suggested that he pay very close attention to the last word.

*

Taking Care Of Business

Includes

Taking Care Of Your "Self"

*

"Forget about work for the time being," Uncle suggested. "We will get back to it. Concentrate on your *'self.'* My 'self' is who I am. Your 'self' is who you are. Our 'selves' are as different as our fingerprints. It is this 'self' that we need to take care of."

The nephew asked, "Why is this so important?"

"Because when we take good care of our 'selves,' we are healthier and happier. And then we work better and are more able to help other people."

Uncle continued, "Some years ago, I began to see happiness more clearly when I looked at the opposite extreme. How do people feel, who are so unhappy that they are severely depressed?"

The man said, "They just don't care—about themselves, others, even their surroundings."

"That's exactly how they feel," Uncle agreed. "They don't care. And how do other people feel when they are around people who just don't care?"

The man smiled and said, "It's depressing."

Uncle laughed, "So people who take very poor care of themselves are clearly not good for others. If they took better care of themselves, would that also be better for others?"

While the man was thinking, Uncle asked, "What's a sign that a depressed patient is recovering?"

The man said, "They start to take better care of themselves. They comb their hair for instance."

Uncle nodded, "Yes. Healthy people take good care of themselves. Unhealthy people do not.

"So what do you think I did?" Uncle asked.

Uncle answered his own question. "I started to see myself as a *caretaker*. You can too, if you like.

"Imagine, if you will," his uncle continued, "that you are the respected caretaker of a beautiful garden on a magnificent estate. People visit your garden from all over the world to admire you and your work.

"In your mind's eye, see the elegant results of your work. Smell the fragrances."

The uncle paused to let the scene sink in. "How does it feel to be such a caretaker?"

The man thought, "It feels good. *I* feel good."

Uncle said, "I feel balanced when I see three major areas in my garden: 'Me,' 'Thee,' and 'We.'"

The nephew said, "You see yourself Taking Care of Me, Taking Care of Thee, and Taking Care of We. Is that what you mean?"

"Yes. 'Me' is my self," Uncle confirmed.

"'Thee,'" Uncle nodded, "is the 'Me' in you. You have the same basic needs I do, so I recognize the needs of your 'Me'. when I think of Thee."

As he touched the world globe that stood in the corner of his study, Uncle said, "And 'We' is the relationship that you and I have —whether 'you' are a member of my family, a business associate, or a stranger on the other side of this globe."

There was peace and energy around Uncle.

The man felt he wanted to know more. "Would you tell me about the first part of your philosophy: 'Taking Care of Me'?"

"Let's go out in the garden," the uncle suggested. "We'll treat ourselves to some sunshine."

The man looked around his uncle's garden. He heard the running water and saw the beautiful flowers. He felt the peace and tranquillity. He was beginning to see how his being a caretaker could nurture him.

Uncle reflected, "Looking at this garden, it's hard to remember when I was so unhappy."

"What was wrong?" the man asked.

"I simply wasn't taking care of myself. At first, I didn't know what was wrong. I didn't even enjoy the success I was having or my family or friends.

"As I took a closer look, I realized that I was taking better care of my business than I was of my family, and better care of my family than I was of myself. I let my life get out of balance."

The man asked, "What did you do?"

"As simple as it sounds, several times every day I began to stop and take One Minute for Myself."

"One minute isn't very long," the man complained.

"It's long enough to become happier," the older man said. "Look at your watch. Now, sit in silence. Don't look at your watch until you feel one minute has passed, not a second more nor less."

Uncle waited while his nephew quietly tried the experiment. He knew what would happen.

After what seemed like a minute, his nephew looked at his watch. He was surprised. "It's only thirty-eight seconds," he said. "A minute is longer than I thought."

His uncle smiled. It happened every time. "When we are quiet, one minute is a long time."

"Why One Minute?" the man asked.

Uncle explained, "Because in one quiet minute with myself, I can first *become aware* of what I am doing and then I can *choose* to see a better way.

"In addition to other things I do to take good care of Me, I also do it for Thee and We. I invest in myself and others that one *extra* minute that makes such a big difference!"

The man asked, "How do you do that?"

Uncle said, "I simply stop and quietly ask, *Is there a better way right now for me to take good care of Me?* As amazing as it seems, it works.

"When I stop for a minute to quietly look, I often see a better way. And then, as often as possible, I do it."

"How do you take care of Thee," the man wanted to know, "in one minute?"

"I encourage Thee—the 'Me' in you—to see that you and I are alike. You also need to take good care of yourself. I invite you to take one minute to stop and gently ask *yourself* the same quiet question: *Is there a way, right now, for me to take better care of myself?*

"Because you, who have your answer within," Uncle said, "deserve to be nurtured as well."

The man asked, "How do you take care of We?"

"I encourage each of us to take the time to quietly ask ourselves, *Am I asking another person or our relationship to do the impossible—to take good care of me—or are we each taking better care of ourselves and thus enjoying an even better relationship together?*

Uncle heard the man's doubt. "How could something so simple be so powerful?"

"Because," Uncle said, "that simple, quick minute of looking at and thinking about my behavior or my thoughts leads on to something very powerful. It leads me within myself to listen to my own wisdom.

"Taking One Minute out a few times a day to stop and look at what I am doing is like driving across town and stopping at the stop signs. The stop signs help me get safely where I want to go."

The man realized, "So just stopping and looking prevents you from running into something and hurting yourself."

"Yes," Uncle said. "I stop, look, and see that I have a choice: to proceed ahead, or change directions, or do whatever I see is best for me.

"And," Uncle added, "I am less likely to run into and hurt *other* people who are also at the intersection with me. It helps me take care of myself *and* others.

"Taking One Minute for Myself, when I remember to do it," Uncle said, "has proved invaluable to me.

"Almost always, I find the answer within me. The truth is we each know what is best, if we will just stop long enough to see it."

The man began to feel that his uncle might well know something worth remembering. He took out pen and paper and asked, "Do you mind if I take a few notes?"

He jotted down the best of what he'd already heard.

Uncle began to explain in detail. "Let's begin at the very beginning with Taking Care of Me. Then we will 'graduate,' as I see it, to a higher level: Taking Care of Thee and finally Taking Care of We. You will see that one builds on the other to provide balance."

The man asked, "What do you do?"

"*What* I do is the easy part," Uncle said. "Once I make the commitment to do something every day to Take Care of Me, I find a variety of ways to do it. I just try to remember to do something for myself as often and as well as I do something for other people.

"Whatever I do for myself, however, lets me feel cared for. And that's what makes me feel happy.

"What *you* do to take care of yourself will probably be different from what I do. In fact, part of the joy of taking better care of yourself, Nephew, will be discovering what works uniquely for you.

"What I do to take care of myself may change from week to week. But it usually begins the same way.

"First, I take that extra minute for myself during the day to stop and ask, 'Is there a better way, right now, for me to take care of Me?'

"Once I've done that, what I do to take care of myself depends on what I am doing or thinking about when I asked myself the question. Usually it leads to a change in my behavior or in my thoughts."

The man asked, "Would you give me some specific examples, Uncle, of how you take care of yourself?"

"Certainly," Uncle said. "I remember when I felt I just didn't have enough time to myself during the day.

"In the middle of feeling resentful about this, I took a minute out. I thought about it quietly for a while, and rather than stay resentful, I decided to get up an hour earlier in the morning and have that be 'my' hour to do with as I liked sometime during the day."

Uncle smiled. "But I remember the first morning I tried it. I was tired and I really didn't want to get up. I remember sleepily asking, 'Isn't there a better way?'

"I decided to get up only fifteen minutes earlier but to do it earlier each week for four weeks. In a month, I had an extra hour a day to myself."

"What do you do with your hour?" the man asked.

"You're missing the point," Uncle said. "It doesn't matter as long as I feel that I am taking care of myself. That's the important thing."

Uncle stressed this by repeating the point.

"It doesn't matter what I do. It's the little things that make a big difference—things maybe nobody else would notice."

Then Uncle said, "One thing I do when I get rushed, feel overwhelmed, and lose my perspective is to ask myself another simple question: 'Ten years from now, how much difference is this going to make?'"

The man nodded. "I'll bet you do fewer unimportant things now and are probably more peaceful."

"That's true," his uncle confirmed.

"Another thing I do for myself," the older man added, "is to laugh. The more often I laugh the healthier and happier I am. I remember hearing a great comedy album on the radio. It made me laugh so hard and I felt so good that I bought some comedy tapes for my car. Now I enjoy driving down the street laughing."

The man said, "I remember when you were too serious. You now laugh more. What happened?"

His uncle responded, "Fortunately, I had a friend who had a great sense of humor. I watched him and saw how humor improved his life. He worked under pressure like I did, but it didn't seem to get to him. So I began to embrace his lighthearted philosophy.

"I remember once when I was down, my friend asked me how I felt. I said I felt like hiding.

"Then he said, 'No problem.' He asked me if I had a closet in my house. I said, 'Of course I do.' He said, 'That's the perfect place.' 'For what?' I asked.

"He said, 'For hiding. Go in your closet, take in a chair, sit down, and close the door.' "

Uncle laughed and said, "I soon saw how amusing my little drama was. Then I didn't need to hang on to it."

"So laughing at yourself is a good way of taking care of yourself," the man noted.

"Yes," Uncle said. "Even better, I laugh *with* myself. I enjoy my follies, my imperfections, and my humanness.

"I do this with a little trick," Uncle added.

"What is that?" the man asked.

"When I take myself too seriously," Uncle said, "I now imagine an amused God in the clouds watching my progress because humans amuse him and because he really likes me.

"All of a sudden, God bursts out laughing. He shouts out to one of his good buddies, 'Come here. You gotta see what Uncle's doing! It's an absolute scream!'"

The man laughed. "I'll remember that."

Uncle said, "Laughing at myself and doing little things for myself really help me feel good."

Uncle continued, "You wanted examples of what I do. Sometimes I skip lunch and change my routine. I go for a walk. Or I shop for some small item for myself—one that lets me feel that I am taking care of myself.

"I may take a drive in my car to look at beautiful scenery. Or go to a concert.

"Sometimes I make appointments with myself in the middle of the day to do something strictly for myself. I remember, once, I even went to an art museum at eleven A.M. Then I went back and worked during my normal lunchtime.

"I go on local expeditions. I take myself into places where I have never been, just to see what I will feel like when I am there. It may be a part of town I don't normally go to, or a shop I've never been in. The change makes me feel more adventurous and alive.

"Those are the little things. But there is something more important."

The older man handed his nephew a plaque he kept on the desk in his study. It read:

*

I Treat Myself
The Way I Would Like Others
To Treat Me

*

"What do you mean?"

"When I think that people do not treat me well," Uncle said, "I look at how I treat myself.

"My life is going well now because I have taken care of myself in these important areas. Sometimes I still start feeling like I'm not getting a fair shake. Usually it's over something small. I still don't like it very much when I feel I'm not being treated well."

"I know how you feel," the young man said.

"But as soon as I stop and see that I'm feeling like a victim," Uncle said, "I know who my persecutor is."

"Yourself?" the man guessed.

"Myself," Uncle confirmed. "Soon I remember that I can be either my best friend or my worst enemy. It all depends on what I choose to think and choose to do."

"What is an example of what you might do?"

"I don't like it when other people feel I don't live up to their expectations of me. So I avoid setting myself up with rigid expectations and comparing me to what I think ought to be. When I am disappointed in myself, it is usually because I didn't get what I demanded of me.

"I have learned not to expect my perfect fantasy Thanksgiving holidays of turkeys, candles, and absolutely grateful family and friends.

"I now see it," Uncle said, "as a time for me to give *thanks* for what I *do* have already."

The man said, "So the disappointment—the unhappiness—is the difference between the fantasy and the reality."

"Yes," Uncle confirmed. "Now I simply appreciate what happens instead of comparing it to what I think ought to happen. I've learned that my personal pain comes from the difference between what is happening and what I think ought to be happening."

The man said, "So if I let go of what I think is missing from the fantasy and appreciate what is already good about the reality, I'll be happier."

"It works for me," his uncle said.

The older man continued, "I take care of me by looking at what I *want* versus what I *need*."

"What is the difference between the two?"

"A need," the older man said, "is something we require for our well-being. A want is something we hope will make us happy—but often does not. I *want* a candy bar. I *need* oxygen.

"It is like success and happiness," Uncle said. "Many successful but unhappy people have discovered that what they pursued and got did not make them happy.

"I feel successful when I get what I want," Uncle said. "But I feel happy when I want what I get.

"Again, I see things more clearly," Uncle explained, "when I stop and look at what I am pursuing."

Uncle paused to let his nephew see the importance of what he was going to say. "We can never, never get enough of what we don't need.

"It's like wanting money, getting it, discovering it doesn't make you happy, and yet wanting more, hoping *that* will make you happy."

"Then how do you know what you need, Uncle?"

"By spending time looking at what really makes *me* happy. Some days I'm in the mood to write things down and analyze them. Other days I go for a walk and listen in silence to myself.

"When I take a minute to ask, 'Do I really need what I am chasing?,' I often stop pursuing it."

The man said, "That reminds me of when I was learning how to hang glide. I saw a boy trying to fly while his instructor yelled up from the ground, 'Watch out for the parked cars. Don't hit that green car! I said don't hit that green . . .' Guess where the guy went?

"Right," he continued, "into the green car. My instructor said, 'Let that be a lesson to you. Never look at where you don't want to go.'

"I'm beginning to understand," the nephew added. "You reduce the stress in your life by not aiming at what you don't need."

"Sure. What do you think you or I would feel if we'd worked hard to get something, only to discover we didn't need it in the first place?"

"I'd be disappointed," the man said, "maybe even depressed. So it really pays to stop and look."

"Exactly! And if I am not willing to take that time to stop and look at what is really best for me, who is?

"It really is very simple. The more I take good care of myself, the more I feel well taken care of."

"What do you do, Uncle, when things aren't going well for you? How do you take care of yourself?"

"I look past the bad until I find the good. You may want to do the same when things look bad."

The man said, "I will try to do that. May I ask what else you do that works for you?"

"Yes. I uncomplicate my life," Uncle said. "It's a quick way to reduce stress. I cut away more and more until I find the core of what makes me happy.

"When I get it simple, I keep it simple. The more simple my life is, the more peaceful it is."

"What do you do to simplify your life, Uncle?"

Again, Uncle challenged him: "I think I'll ask you to think about what you can do to uncomplicate *your* life."

Uncle stood up and walked around. "I'm going to give you a little more of my time this morning and then I'm going to go play."

"Play?" the man asked.

Uncle answered, "Playing is like laughing. It, too, is one of the ways I take care of myself.

"Play is for the body what a good attitude is for the mind. As for play, I like to play tennis with my buddies and go skinny-dipping with your aunt."

The nephew smiled. "I think you'd like a friend of mine. His life isn't without problems, but he's got a great attitude. He thinks life is a game.

"Before he opens his eyes in the morning, he always stretches his arms out all around him. He says if he can't feel the sides of a coffin, he knows it's gonna be a good day!"

Uncle laughed. "Attitude is the name of the game. How you look at life is the single best way to take care of yourself. You have a perspective that either beats you up or builds you up. And we can *choose* our attitude.

"As I've grown older, and I hope smarter," Uncle added, "it seems to me that there are really only two basic emotions in my life. The two emotions are Love (positive) and Fear (negative). One is the absence of the other. It may be that all the other emotions are a variation of one of these two."

"What about anxiety?" the man asked.

Uncle answered, "Anxiety is fear of the unknown.

"Whenever I am not taking care of myself," Uncle admitted, "I realize that I am operating out of fear.

"When I choose to operate out of love," he added, "I feel cared for. I feel happy.

"So when I make a decision," Uncle said, "I ask, 'Is this a love-filled decision or a fearful decision'?

Decisions I make based on fear, whether I am aware of it or not, do not turn out very well for me."

The man admitted to himself that his hadn't either.

"When I make a decision based on love (the absence of fear)," Uncle continued, "I feel good—even before I know the outcome.

"Another way I take care of myself is by giving away part of my time and my money."

"How is that an example of taking care of yourself?"

"Because," Uncle said, "when I give away some of my money or my time, it reminds me that I am not afraid. I believe I will always have enough to share with others."

Uncle added, "When I *am* afraid, I still try to choose non-fearful decisions anyway. I love that feeling of *deciding* I am not going to be afraid."

Uncle seemed so clear, the man wondered if *he* would ever learn how to take care of *himself*.

As though he could read his nephew's concern, Uncle said, "Let me tell you a true story. When he was a young man, our neighbor didn't know whether to take a job he'd been offered in New York. So he asked the advice of a wise old gentleman he admired.

"The old man advised, 'Go alone to New York. Travel all the way across the country by train. Take nothing with you to read and nothing with which to write. Get a private compartment. Have the porter bring you all your meals. Speak to no one. That is my advice.'

"My neighbor tells me he soon regretted agreeing to follow the old man's advice. But he did as advised.

"After a few days, he got bored looking at the scenery. Then what do you think he did?"

"He started to think?" the man asked.

"Of course," Uncle said. "He stopped long enough to take care of himself—to let the answer come to him. By the time he got to New York, he knew he should take the job. He did and he became very successful."

"So he had the answer within him, all the time."

"Sure. And the old man knew he would discover it.

"When our neighbor took time out to stop and spend quiet moments with himself, he saw how best to take good care of himself. It also helped him take better care of his family. The same is true for us.

"We each know what is good for us. We just need to slow down long enough to take care of ourselves.

"Now, guess what I am going to advise you to do?"

The man smiled and said, "Somehow, Uncle, I think I'm going to take a kind of train ride— alone."

PART I

Taking Care of Me

A WEEK had passed since the man had driven away from his uncle's home. But he was not as happy as he had hoped he would be.

He had read over the notes he'd taken during the important conversation with his uncle. But he found it was one thing to talk about taking One Minute for Myself. It was quite another thing to *do* it.

The man simply hadn't done it.

"Maybe, I don't believe it will work," he thought as he drove along in his car. "Or maybe it just takes a little self-discipline."

Changing was more difficult than he had anticipated. The man had to admit he did not like to change. But he also knew that if he wanted to be happier he was going to have to change something.

He decided to read over his notes again and see what it was he would try to do.

In the meantime, he turned off the radio and thought about what he had heard from his uncle.

For some reason, he remembered that Uncle had said that one of the things *he* did in his life was to . . .

*

Simplify

*

Uncle had said that he kept reducing things to their most simple and basic truths.

But the man believed that life was more complicated than that. He certainly saw his own life as difficult and complex. And so he had difficulty with this idea.

However, since he was unable to reread his notes while he was still driving, he decided to try to recall the most simple and fundamental thing that his uncle was saying.

He remembered the ideas of seeing the difference between what he wanted and what he needed, and between expecting the fantasy and enjoying the reality. And he remembered other things that seemed to be an important part of becoming happier.

But they didn't seem so simple. "What is the most simple idea I could use right away?" he tried to recall.

At that moment he approached a stop sign. Then he smiled. He remembered what the simple idea was: to stop, look, and listen. Stop for one minute; ask himself how he could take better care of himself; listen to his own inner wisdom. That was something he could do now.

The man saw that there was no one behind him. So he sat there for a full minute.

He stopped and asked himself, "What is the best way for me right now to take better care of Me?"

He silently listened to himself.

As the man looked through the dirty windshield at the stop sign, he frowned. "I've got to get this car washed someday," he thought.

The man felt better when he was driving a clean car. In fact, a dirty, unorganized, unkempt car made the man feel a little that way himself, though most of the time he wasn't aware of it. But he felt he was just too busy to take the time to get it washed.

The man realized that he had been meaning to get the car washed for some time, or at least to put some fluid in the windshield washer. Usually he thought he had other things to do. So he ignored it.

But he wound up looking at a dirty view and feeling that he hadn't done what would have made him happier.

The man looked out through his dirty windshield, saw it was safe to proceed, and drove away from the stop sign. He already knew what he was going to do.

He just wondered why he hadn't done it earlier.

He took the time to drive to a gas station with a car wash, get the car washed, and have the windshield washer filled. He called his wife to let her know what he was doing and that he would be a little late.

When he offered to pay with his major credit card, he found it was not acceptable. The attendant was firm about it. He wanted cash.

In the past, something like this at the end of a long work day would have annoyed him.

But he was feeling good. He was glad he had taken the time to do something for himself. And the car gleamed—they had done a good job.

The man smiled, paid in cash, and drove away.

The man thought, "It's amazing how a small thing like cleaning my car can make a big difference." He looked out his clean windshield and smiled. "I see the world differently when I take better care of myself."

The man usually came home feeling the stress of work. He'd have a drink and watch TV.

That night, however, he decided to read a book about a simple relaxation technique to reduce stress.

He had gotten out of the habit of reading and so he read only part of the book. Then he watched television with his wife and children. It was relaxing but boring.

The next night, however, he finished the book. At first he was disappointed because it described a very simple technique indeed.

He wondered if it would work. But a few nights later, he found a quiet place and sat in a chair with both feet on the floor and his eyes closed. He breathed in and out deeply and slowly.

Then, in his mind, he quietly repeated the word "one" over and over again. He tried to think of nothing else but the word "one." He could feel himself relaxing.

When other thoughts came into the man's mind, he just gently replaced these distracting thoughts by easily repeating the word "one" in his mind. He did this for about twenty minutes.

At first he didn't see such wonderful results. But he repeated this simple relaxation method each morning before he went to work and again each evening. Then something happened.

He didn't know when it happened, but he realized, at some point, that he'd become more relaxed. He had far less tension in his neck and shoulders. The man felt less stress.

He reread parts of the book again. The more he studied and used the relaxing method, the less stress he felt. And the more peaceful he became.

He decided to continue to use the relaxing technique.

The following week, the man left for a multi-city business trip. Because it was an important trip, he was accompanied by two of his business associates.

The flight from Boston was delayed. They were scheduled to arrive in Los Angeles at 9 P.M.— midnight Boston time. But the plane was two hours late departing. He and the others thought they would arrive at 2 A.M. "their time."

They all knew about the important meeting early the next morning. So each was anxious to get into his hotel room and get some rest. But the West Coast airport was fogged in. As they descended, the man felt the plane suddenly lift back up into the air.

They later learned that this was done to avoid another airplane in the fog. He and the others were told they were going to have to land in San Diego—over one hundred miles away.

They would then have to take a three-hour bus ride to their hotel. They would be lucky to be in their beds at all before the important meeting.

The man felt exhausted. Then he did something to take better care of himself.

Riding in the bus, he had been angrily thinking about what had happened. If the plane had left on time, maybe he would have arrived before the fog set in. Or maybe they could have landed in the fog and avoided the long bus ride.

The man felt the fatigue. He thought he would never be able to do well in the meeting feeling so tired. He didn't feel exactly nurtured—far from it.

Then he stopped for a minute and asked himself if there was a better way for him to nurture himself. There was little he could do about the circumstances. So he looked at what he could control: his thinking.

He knew the loss of time was annoying him. So the man chose to see his circumstances differently. He saw himself not wasting time on the bus. He saw himself instead in the plane crash that could have happened in the dangerous fog. And the man soon figured out that an airplane crash would have taken up a whole lot more than just his time. Pretty soon he was delighted to be riding along in a nice comfortable bus.

It was at that moment, riding on a bus at night in Southern California, that he realized what Uncle had been talking about.

There was something the man could do in just one minute—something that could change *everything*.

*

In One Minute
You Can Change Your Attitude

And In That Minute
You Can Change Your Entire Day

*

The man had forgotten what Uncle had said—that one of the things that helped him be happier was to see past the apparent bad to the good in a situation. Yet the man had done that by simply asking and listening to his own inner wisdom. He had discovered the value of a good attitude by himself. And he was happier.

The man was amazed that he was so mentally rested for his meeting. When he saw how much better he did than his tired associates, he promised that he would share his knowledge with them if they should ever ask. But they didn't ask.

It was a quiet breakthrough for the man. He was often told that it helped to have a good attitude.

But he used to get annoyed when people would say such things as "The dark minute the caterpillar calls the end of the world is the sun-filled moment the butterfly calls the beginning."

He was beginning to see it had some merit.

Now he knew the value of having a good attitude. He was *doing* it.

In spite of his doubts, the man thought, "Taking One Minute for Yourself really works. It lets me tap into a wise part of me."

And so the man began to do it more often.

One morning, when the man was home showering and scratching an area behind his ear, he remembered a minor rash that had been bothering him for months. Every now and then it itched and irritated the man.

The rash was back but he ignored it.

Then he stopped for a minute.

He smiled and asked himself if there wasn't a better way for him to take care of himself.

He soon knew what to do. It was obvious. He'd just never taken the time to do it.

He took a minute to telephone for an appointment with a dermatologist, whom he saw three days later.

Emerging from the doctor's office where he had spent forty-five minutes, the man was already feeling better about himself.

A diagnosis had been made, an effective medicine had been applied, and the itch was already gone. The man was also assured that if he used this medicine a few times a day, the rash would clear up.

And he learned that whenever he stopped using the harsh chemicals found in "the wrong kind" of shampoo he used for his hair, he would most likely never have this problem again.

He wondered why he hadn't started taking good care of himself sooner—and more often.

Sometimes, however, the man forgot to *do* what he now knew would work well for him.

He realized, therefore, that he would have to make a disciplined effort to change. And he knew that one of the best ways to change his behavior was to *repeatedly* take one minute for himself over and over until one day it would come easily and naturally for him.

It would become a better way of life.

He had learned and re-learned to stop for one minute a few times during his day to look more closely at what he was doing or what he was thinking.

Then he asked himself, "How can I take better care of Me right now?"

He listened and he usually found an answer.

It certainly took more than a minute, the man realized, for him to take good care of himself. But he now saw what Uncle was talking about.

"Taking One Minute for Yourself," he thought, "leads me to think better and do things better than I used to."

He was discovering many ways to take good care of himself. And he felt better for it.

Over the month, the man changed.

He felt happier.

But as well as it worked, the man was disappointed that he often forgot to do it.

He was reminded of the story about the little kid who came home from his first day in school and his mother and dad asked him if he had learned very much that day. The little kid said, "Naw, I got to go back again tomorrow."

That was how the man felt. Every day it seemed he had to re-learn how to take better care of himself.

He knew, however, that he would do it more and more frequently. Because he knew it worked.

He wondered, however, *why* it worked so well.

THE weeks passed quickly for the man. He had doubted that it would work but had done what his uncle suggested.

He had begun to balance his life. He was learning to take as good care of himself as he took of other parts of his life, including his business and his family.

And he was happier than he had been in a long time.

"Thank you, Uncle," he said as he entered the man's home. "What you told me about Taking Care of Me really works.

"I have already begun to feel happier and healthier.

"I have more energy. Even my disposition has improved. I enjoy life more."

But he wondered why it was so. He asked two questions.

"First, if it works as well as it does, why haven't I, and so many other people I know, taken better care of ourselves sooner?

"And second, why does it work so well?"

"To begin with," said his uncle, "we all used to do a very good job of taking good care of ourselves. When we were infants, we demanded what we needed and we got it. Our first words included 'me,' 'I,' 'want.'

"Then we began to think about other people. We learned words like 'you,' 'they,' 'we,' 'us.'

"It is our natural progression: to think of ourselves, and then to go past ourselves and think about others. It is just as true when we are adults.

"Let me ask you a question," the uncle said.

"Whom do you think about most of the time?"

The man thought for a moment and then looked a little embarrassed. "Myself," he admitted.

Uncle said, "We all think mostly about ourselves. That's normal and natural. When we do this without guilt, we *automatically* go on to think of others. But most of us are afraid this is selfish.

"When we were young, other well-intentioned people became afraid for us. They feared that if we thought too much about ourselves, we would never go on to think of the interests of others. They knew such egotism doesn't work in life.

"So, rather than trust us to care about ourselves, and go on to care about others, they asked us to reverse the natural order: to put others first and ourselves last, like putting the cart before the horse.

"Imagine that others are 'the cart,' which you have placed in front of you, 'the horse.' Now imagine you and the others trying hard to get someplace with this arrangement. Try harder! Do you feel the frustration?"

Uncle asked, "Does that work for anyone?"

The man recognized, "No. So if I can't arrange things in their natural order, I can't make much progress."

Uncle said, "Exactly. But on the road to happiness, so to speak, we all too often put others first and ourselves last. This doesn't get us very far. We are stalled."

The nephew asked, "If it is natural for us to think of ourselves first, why do we feel guilty about doing it?"

"Let's go back and look briefly at our childhoods," Uncle suggested. "Do you remember how you drew a picture of a face when you were a little kid?"

Without waiting the uncle noted, "Look at your own child's drawings today and you will see that the nose is drawn as two little round circles."

"Sure," the man laughed. "When I was little and looking up at my parents, they seemed as tall as a giant sequoia tree. All I saw was the bottom of the nose: the nostrils—two round holes."

"And from that perspective," the uncle noted, "we listened to a lot of well-intentioned information from our folks. What they said from above made an impact.

"Often they told us that it was bad to think so much of ourselves. After all, who were we?

"In fact, we were told it so often when we were young, that I'll bet you," the uncle challenged, "that I cannot start the following sentence without your finishing it."

"What is the sentence?" the man asked.

Uncle asked, "Just who . . . do you think . . ."

"You are?!!!" the man completed the sentence.

"Oh," Uncle laughed. "You've heard it."

His uncle mockingly said, "Of course, I've never said something that dumb to my children. Oh no.

"Here's another one. See if it sounds familiar.

"Don't you ever . . . think of anyone . . ."

"Besides . . . yourself?!!" his nephew finished.

"Sure. Our parents were just trying to instill in us a consideration for other people.

"But what did most of us hear? We heard that we should put others before ourselves.

"So guess where we feel we end up, when we place ourselves last?" his uncle asked.

"Last," the man said with a sigh.

"Yes. Do you remember how it felt as a youngster when you continually put your interests behind others'?"

The man said, "I didn't like it. I *still* don't."

"Nobody does," Uncle noted, "if they are honest with themselves. We knew it as children. It is a natural knowledge we each have.

"Our parents were understandably concerned that we would become little monsters running roughshod over other people's feelings. And so, in their zeal to make sure we were wise enough to consider other people, they forgot to give us the same courtesy.

"When we heard it often enough, we began to put ourselves at the end of the line." Then Uncle asked, "Have you ever heard of the Yellow Elephant effect?"

The man smiled and said, "Not yet."

"You're about to," Uncle chuckled, "whether you want to or not. It will let you learn a simple truth about your unconscious mind. Please do as I tell you: 'Do not, I repeat, do not think about yellow elephants.'"

His nephew started to laugh.

"Do not think about even one yellow elephant— let alone a herd of yellow elephants running across the dusty plains of Africa.

"Now, what have you been thinking about?"

The man smiled. "Yellow elephants."

"You see," Uncle noted, "our subconscious mind has no filter on it. It lets in every image, even if it is unreal. Some of our beliefs are no more real than yellow elephants, but they are dancing in our minds.

"What we hear from other people comes into our minds as pictures. And what we see and hear often enough, we tend to believe."

Uncle said, "We often believe at least two things that work against us.

"One, we mistakenly believe that we should always put others first and ourselves last. The truth is we need to *balance* our interests equally with those of others.

"Two, we often believe that we do not deserve to think of ourselves. The truth is we *do*.

"Now," Uncle said excitedly, "let's take a more uplifting and happier view of what life can be like. Think back on the last weeks when you took better care of yourself. Were you less angry?"

"Yes! My wife and others commented on it."

Uncle said, "The reason it works is simple:

*

*When You Take Good Care Of
Yourself You Feel Less Angry
—Toward Yourself And Others.*

*And When You Are Happier
You Work Better And
You Treat Others Better.*

*

Uncle said, "You are not as angry because you are finally doing what always made sense to you in the first place. You are getting your life in balance by taking as good care of yourself as you are of others. So you are no longer as frustrated.

"It is not surprising that others also find you less angry. You are probably no longer blaming them for what you were doing to yourself."

The man said, "You know, that really makes good sense to me. That is how I have felt lately.

"But why," the man asked, "does the One Minute approach work so well? It's so simple I find it hard to understand why it is so powerful."

Uncle answered, "One Minute for Yourself is a simple application in modern life of an ancient wisdom.

"It has been described by many people in different cultures over the ages, including those in China, India, and the Middle East. Zen philosophers call this the power of *self-observation.*

"It is the ability each of us has and few of us use. The power of self-observation begins in a moment of silence. With this method, it is one minute. This merely begins the process of course.

"In this quiet time, we can begin to *see* what we are doing—or thinking. We can observe our *selves.*"

The man realized, "And when we *see* . . . what we do . . . we can then . . . *change* what we are doing. Is that it?"

"That's almost it," Uncle said. "It is not so much that we can *change* what we are doing. It is more that we can *choose* what we are doing.

"We may choose to change," Uncle said, "or not to change. The point is that in one simple minute, we can observe our behavior or our thoughts.

"Then we can choose our next behavior or our next thought. We can begin to take better care of ourselves. But this is only the beginning."

The man asked, "Is it just the beginning because it starts a larger process?"

"Exactly," Uncle agreed. "The One Minute can open into a larger world for each of us."

"What world?" the man asked.

Uncle answered, "The quiet world you enter is your own inner world—your *self*. Again, it has been called by many names throughout the ages. But to me, it is as simple as the name I use for it: My Best Self. Whatever you want to call it, the power—and it is very powerful—comes from taking the time to be quiet and listen to this Best Self."

The man asked, "What is My Best Self?"

"Within each of us is a part of us that knows what is 'best' for us. However, modern man, and that includes us," Uncle noted, "goes so fast that we race right past ourselves, ignoring all the warning signs that tell us we are off track and that we need to get back on course.

"It's when we take the time to stop, look, and listen to ourselves that we find what is best for *us*.

"That is why it pays," Uncle said, "to do something as simple as spending one special minute with our better selves. In that minute we can begin to see ourselves.

"Every day we have opportunities to take care of ourselves and others if we will just look."

The nephew said, "That reminds me of a story."

Uncle smiled. He was pleased that his nephew seemed to be taking life less seriously.

"This man was stranded on his rooftop as dangerous floodwaters rose around him. Lots of people came to offer help, but he refused to leave his home, saying, 'I'm a good man. God will save me.'

"Unfortunately, he drowned. And was he annoyed!

"When he went to heaven, he complained, 'God, why didn't you save me?' God said, 'I sent you a log, two boats, and a helicopter.' God shrugged his shoulders and said, 'With some people, it's never enough.'"

The uncle laughed. "That's good. When we do not take good care of ourselves, other people can never do enough to make us happy."

"I must admit," the man said, "as simple as it is, when I do this, I am able to bring out the best in me."

"And when we bring out the best in ourselves," Uncle noted, "whom do we also bring out the best in?"

"Others?" the man asked.

"Absolutely," Uncle confirmed. "In fact, one of the greatest joys I get from taking care of myself is discovering that it is also the best way for me to help other people. When I do, we all win.

"But that is the subject for another day."

T HE man reflected on all he had heard. He wove his own thoughts in among his uncle's.

"Thank you, Uncle," the younger man said, "for sharing your wisdom with me.

"Or better yet," he noted, "for helping me discover my own wisdom. I can see now the need to balance taking better care of myself equally with taking good care of others. And I feel better for it."

Then the man had a thought. "Uncle, do you, by any chance, have a simple written summary of all this?"

"Yes, I do," Uncle responded. "When I was first learning how to take care of myself, it was invaluable for me to read and reread my summary.

"In fact, the reason for my written summary is to quickly remind me of what to do when I'm unhappy.

"I must caution you that there are still times when I forget to do what I know works. Then I don't have peace of mind either. *The secret is in the doing.*"

The man knew what his uncle was talking about.

"May I have a copy of the summary?" the man asked. Uncle agreed.

The older man opened his wallet and passed his nephew a small card entitled *One Minute for Myself.*

:01® Taking Care of Me: A Summary

What It Is:

- The greatest reason for outer success—at work and in life—is inner success.

- I realize that taking care of business, means taking care of my "Self."

- To begin with, I simplify my life.

- I treat myself the way I would like others to treat me. I am good to myself.

- I often stop during the day for One Minute to look and listen.

- I look at what I am thinking or what I am doing and ask myself, "How can I take good care of myself?"

- I quietly listen for an answer within me—to the wisdom of my Best Self and discover what is really best for me.

- When I *clearly* see what is best for me, I usually do it.

Why It Works:

- When I take good care of myself, I am less angry and happier—with myself and others.

- When I am happier, I work better. And I treat the people around me better.

PART II

Taking Care of Thee

R ETURNING to his uncle's home the following Saturday morning, the man exclaimed, "I can't get over the difference. Since I've started to take better care of myself, I am happier and more peaceful. I have more energy, and I get more work done. I feel great!"

Uncle was pleased. But he knew better.

"I know how good you feel," Uncle said. "I felt the same exhilaration when I first gave myself permission to take very good care of myself.

"But don't you feel that something is missing?" his uncle challenged.

The man was disappointed that his uncle had taken the edge off his happiness. So he asked himself, "Can I be doing something better for me right now than feeling disappointment?" Then he chose to hear his uncle's enthusiasm as Uncle recalled how good it was for him too.

After that, he thought about why his uncle had tempered his reaction. What else could he learn?

"Now that you mention it," the man admitted, "something does feel missing—incomplete."

Uncle suggested, "Remember the three areas of the garden we spoke of in our first conversation: Taking Care of 'Me'; Taking Care of 'Thee'; and Taking Care of 'We.' You have yet to take care of 'Thee' or 'We.' Therefore, you feel incomplete."

His Uncle picked up a piece of paper. He was writing for a long while. Finally he handed it to his nephew and suggested, "Imagine this:

*

*Thinking Only Of Yourself Is
Like Having Your Favorite Meal*

*Meal . . . After . . . Meal . . . After
. . . Meal . . . After
Meal . . . After . . . Meal . . . After
. . . Meal . . . After . . .*

*

"I got it. I got it," the man said. "That could get sickening and boring fast."

His uncle smiled and asked, "Sickening and boring for whom?"

"For me," the man said. "And . . ." he then realized, "for those around me."

"So what do you think the answer is?" Uncle asked.

The man realized, "The answer seems to be for me to balance my thinking about myself . . . with . . . somehow taking good care of others. I guess, as good care as I take of myself.

"Taking better care of myself," the man said, "as I've learned to do in these past few weeks, has worked very well for me. I feel happier and peaceful.

"But I wonder what effect it has on other people."

"Why don't you find out?" Uncle suggested.

"How?" the man asked.

His uncle smiled but said nothing.

The man responded, "You want me to figure that out for myself. Let's see . . .

"You certainly take care of yourself, Uncle. I suppose I could talk to people who know you. And then see what effect it has on them."

As soon as Uncle suggested it, the man knew whom he wanted to talk to: the business people who worked with Uncle and, perhaps later, the one person who knew Uncle best.

The man stood up and shook hands with his favorite uncle. He sensed it was time to move beyond an interest in himself.

U NCLE'S business associate greeted the man in her office. "So you want to know how taking good care of yourself affects other people."

He thought, "She certainly gets right to the heart of the matter. No wonder she's in charge."

"Your uncle has really helped me," she said. "If I can help you, I'd be happy to do so.

"Several years ago, your uncle taught a lot of us around here a very important lesson.

"He used to be my boss's boss. And frankly he also used to be a real pain." The man was startled.

"But that was a very long time ago. Then something extraordinary happened. He became more pleasant.

"And his work, as good as it already was, improved dramatically. None of us could figure out what had happened to him.

"Eventually we worked up the courage to ask.

"Instead of telling us, he asked us questions, as though we had the answers."

The nephew laughed. He knew what she meant.

"Your uncle asked, 'How much time do you spend taking care of yourself? Do you take better care of your job than you do of yourself?'

"We admitted that we didn't take very good care of ourselves. We were busy doing other things.

"Then he told us that he had started to give himself more time and attention—as much as he was giving to others—including those in his family and his business. We were surprised."

"Why were you surprised?" the man asked.

"Because we noticed that he was doing a much *better* job of taking care of his business. And he was getting along so much better with other people. It looked like just the opposite of what he was saying.

"He told us that the reason for this was that he was taking better care of himself.

"That," she said, "got our attention.

"Later he told us he'd discovered that the way he treated others was the way he treated himself. He challenged me to look at my relationships.

"I saw how taking care of himself had improved your uncle's relationship with others.

"So I thought about it. I admitted to him and to me that I was very critical of people. And they didn't like that very much. He asked me whom I criticized most.

"I admitted, 'I'm most critical of myself.'

"He suggested that I take better care of myself and then asked where I thought I might begin."

The woman and young man both knew the answer. "So I began to take a minute for myself.

"Whenever I began to criticize something about me, I would take one minute to simply stop, look, and ask myself, 'Is there . . .'"

The man completed, "Is there a better way to take care of myself right now?"

"Exactly. You know, it's amazing how much just stopping, looking, and asking myself that question has helped me. My relationships with other people have improved tremendously at work and at home."

"What did you do?"

"Whenever I started to criticize myself, I would stop and look at what I was doing to Me. Then I chose to replace my critical thought of me with a thought of something I liked about myself.

"Or when I really didn't like my behavior, I would criticize my *behavior* but never my *self*. When I saw that what I was *doing* was not who I *was*, it was soon easier for me to let go of what I was doing."

"And then what happened?"

"I started to feel better about myself. I began to work better—both alone and with others."

"Was it that easy?" the man asked.

"No, not at first. It was hard for me to get into the habit of taking that one minute for myself. It was only when I stopped and took the one minute out a few times a day, every day, that things improved."

The man thought about how often during the day he took one minute for himself. "Even five times a day adds up to only five minutes." He decided to do it even more often.

"How did things get better for you?"

"Once I stopped criticizing myself, I stopped criticizing others.

"Then I got along better with other people at work and we accomplished more. We got greater results in less time. It's amazing how fast it happened.

"The word got around and soon others were taking one minute for themselves. Evidently they got the same results."

"What do you mean?" the man asked.

"Our general manager in those days called us together and told us that we had almost doubled our departmental profits! He asked what was going on.

"When we told him, I think he was in shock. He smiled and said, 'Whatever works . . .'

"Later we heard that he had started to take one minute for himself."

"And why not," the man noted, "if it works!"

"The irony is that I spent more time taking care of myself," she said, "and less time taking care of others.

"And yet both my business and other people benefited. How practical can you get?"

His uncle's business associate added, "He's your real uncle, but he's also been a Dutch uncle to us, telling us what we needed to hear for our own good. And now that enough of us are taking better care of ourselves, business is booming.

"And it's not just the business that wins," she added.

The woman looked around her large corner office, spread her hands wide, and said, "As you can see, taking One Minute for Yourself now and then throughout the day has paid off." She was obviously proud of what she had learned to do.

"I am happier at home and more successful at work," she said, "since I learned the most important lesson of all from your uncle.

"He taught me that the key to my taking good care of other people was to help them take care of themselves. I keep this plaque on my desk to remind me:

*

*One Of The Best Ways
You Can Help Other People*

*Is To Encourage Them
To Take Better Care Of
Themselves*

*And To Reward Them
When They Do*

*

The woman said, "Since I've become more aware of this very obvious fact, I have encouraged everyone around me—from my husband and children to my business associates—to take better care of themselves.

"Those of us who get the most work done around here are nurturing ourselves."

"What do you do?" the visitor asked.

"Let's say we have personal goals of wanting more energy or a better figure or to laugh more. We do something before we begin work each day to take care of ourselves.

"Maybe it's getting exercise that morning or taking vitamins. We do something special for ourselves.

"It doesn't matter what we do to take good care of ourselves. It's just the great feeling we get when we know that we are honoring ourselves enough. We're at least as important as our work. Of course we often take one minute for ourselves as we work too—to get a better perspective, to get back into balance when we're frustrated by a problem. It's amazing how quickly that helps you see the issues clearly.

"I am learning that it pays off for me to encourage the other people to take better care of themselves.

"When I do a really good job of taking care of myself, it's really the best way I know of taking care of others."

"Why is that?" the man wanted to know.

The woman said, "Why not ask my husband?"

NOON rang out on the plaza bells as the man approached the artist's studio. . The businesswoman had phoned her husband and he had agreed to meet the man for lunch.

The painter, who was just changing out of his smock, had some fresh fruit and sandwiches brought in.

"I'm glad you came," the artist said. "Talking with you about why taking care of Thee works just gives me a chance to see the beauty of it again for myself.

"Ever since I've done what my wife encouraged me to do—start caring for myself—I've been doing more things for myself. The funny part of it is that others tell me lately that I've been treating them better too. So I've thought a lot about it.

"I tried what my wife suggested because I knew she was taking care of herself and I saw the effect it had.

"At first I didn't like her doing it because I thought I might get left out. But later I noticed that she became more attentive to me than she used to be.

"Pretty soon I'd started saying, 'Hey, you gotta take care of yourself more often. This is great.'

"I started to think about why people taking care of themselves works so well for others around them.

"I told my ideas to your uncle once and he agreed.

"When we successfully take care of our own needs, we are satisfied with ourselves. And then we *want* to turn our attention to others. It's not that we have to. We want to. It feels good.

"Then we can encourage other people to take care of themselves and we reward them when they do. That really pleases them.

"Everybody loves both to be around people who are taking good care of themselves, and to be given permission (as though they really need it) to take good care of themselves."

"Isn't it sometimes difficult," the man asked, "for you to remember to let the other people take care of themselves—especially if you really want them to give *you* their attention?"

"It used to be," the artist admitted, "until I saw one monumental advantage to me."

"An advantage to you?" the visitor asked.

"Yes. A very practical advantage to me."

"What are you talking about?" the visitor asked.

The artist stood up and with mock flair painted his point on his canvas. Then he turned it around to show the man.

All the words but one were painted in black. The last word was underlined and painted in red.

He made his point:

*

When Other People
Take Good Care Of
Themselves

They Are Happier
With Themselves—

And With <u>Me</u>!

*

The man said, "I never thought about that. But you are right. My uncle, for instance, is a lot nicer to me than he used to be."

"Think about it," the artist suggested. "Hasn't that happened since your uncle started being a lot nicer to himself?"

"Yes," the man realized. "So if I want to be treated better by other people, I should encourage them to treat *themselves* better. Because the better they treat themselves, the better they treat others. That's great."

"That's it," the artist confirmed. "That's why it really is to our advantage to help other people consider themselves more in order to bring out the best in themselves. Then we get to enjoy their Best Selves."

The artist said, "My wife was smart enough to know that. Since she has taught me to do it, it has made a big difference in my life. And therefore in her life.

"When we take care of ourselves, we are really taking very good care of others."

The man thought for a moment and then said, "That reminds me of a seemingly small incident that happened to me yesterday, but it makes me realize the importance of what you are saying."

"What was that?" the artist asked.

"I had been running around shopping, getting things for my family. I did take care of myself though, and bought myself a new music cassette. I put everything in the trunk, got into the car to drive home. I was running late and was in a real hurry.

"No sooner had I driven away from the shopping center than I realized how much I wanted to listen to my new music cassette, but it meant stopping and getting it out of the trunk, and I felt I just didn't have the time. My family was expecting me home.

"Then I realized that I could easily start feeling as if I had been doing everything that day for everybody else. Then I asked myself . . .

"'Is there a better way right now for me to take care of Me?' I soon knew there was.

"So I pulled over to the curb, opened the trunk, got out my new music cassette, unwrapped it, and inserted it into my tape deck. Then I continued driving home happily listening to my music."

"Let me guess what happened," the artist said. "As you drove home, you felt good, you were happy.

"If you hadn't pulled over, but had just dashed home, you would have felt that, once again, you took better care of everybody else than you did of yourself. And you would have arrived home in lousy form."

"That's right," the nephew admitted. "I would have felt like a *victim*." Then he laughed at his folly.

The artist said, "Let me guess what happened.

"By taking care of yourself first with something as small as listening to your new music, you arrived home feeling happy and energized. Not only did you look forward to seeing your family and arrive there in a better mood, but they were delighted to feel that as you came in the door. And you all had a more enjoyable evening together."

The man was amazed. "How did you know?"

"I've been there myself," the artist said. "Not the same way, but I know the feeling."

The artist said to the man, "You are like a lot of us who are learning this new way.

"You are teaching yourself that by taking better care of yourself, you really are giving others around you a great gift—a happier and more enjoyable you.

"Speaking of taking good care of myself . . ." the artist said, looking at his unfinished canvas.

The man smiled and said, "I understand.

"I know that you want to get back to your painting and I'm going to leave.

"I also understand a lot more now about how taking care of myself is also the best way to take care of others. It's the best of both worlds.

"Thank you for caring enough about others to spend this time with me. You have been a great help."

The man and the artist clasped hands and parted. As soon as he could he wanted to write down a summary of what he had learned. He wanted to remember it.

The man knew where he was going next.

AS the man drove away from the artist's studio, he realized how important it was to think—really think—about *other* people.

He thought he'd been considerate of other people. In fact, he usually cared more about what other people thought of him than what he thought of himself. It was what other people thought of *him* that concerned him most.

He now realized that what was important to others was not what they thought of *him*, but what they thought of *themselves*.

He saw it was a high priority for other people to feel more kindly toward themselves because it helped them be less angry with themselves. And therefore, less angry with him.

The man stopped at another stop sign.

This time he saw things differently. He realized it was in his own best interests that other people stop and take care of themselves as well.

Otherwise they would run into and hurt him— even though they might not *intend* him any harm.

Then the man had an insight of his own.

More than just encouraging the people close to him to stop and take care of themselves, he would *reward* them when they did.

When his wife or children stopped and found a better way to take good care of themselves, he would reward them with praise.

He pulled over to the side of the road to make notes while these ideas were fresh in his mind.

:01 *Taking Care of Thee: A Summary*

- Thee is "me" in *you*. We are basically alike—you and I. When I remember this, I can help *you* take better care of you.

- I know your taking good care of yourself is as helpful to you as my taking care of myself is to me. Because when you do, you are happier.

- When you are happier, other people—including *me*—are happier when we are with you.

- I show you best *by example* just how good it is for me and for people around me when I stop to take better care of myself.

- I feel balanced and caring when I am helping others take better care of themselves—when I am there for them to help them do it.

- When you take very good care of yourself, you—like me—are also helping take good care of others.

- I encourage you to take that important One Minute for *your* "self": to stop and look at what you are doing or thinking and ask yourself if there is a better way for you.

PART III

Taking Care of We

WALKING along with Auntie, as Uncle and everyone else called her, brought back memories for the man. He could still remember the pies she baked when he had visited her with his parents.

But the nephew didn't remember his aunt and uncle as a close couple. "Auntie, you seem to enjoy a great relationship with Uncle. Do you?"

She turned as she walked and answered, "Yes, I do."

She seemed to be savoring her thoughts.

Then she stopped. "But it wasn't always that way. Don't you remember? Maybe you were too young.

"There was a time when he was too busy taking care of his business. And I guess I was too busy taking care of the children. We weren't taking enough notice of each other. And we most certainly weren't taking good care of ourselves.

"We were both disappointed in our relationship. What we had wasn't what each of us wanted."

"What did you each want?" the nephew asked.

Auntie laughed. "Just everything! We wanted to have the other person take care of us; to feel our pain and our joys; to feel free and bonded to each other at the same time; not to be judged; to be respected; to know that things wouldn't always go well, but to get past the arguments to the love; to be there for each other when we needed support; to care; to be *loved*."

She continued to stroll in silence. Then she said, "We wanted what I suppose most couples dream about.

"We each wanted to be held; to be nurtured; to feel excitement with one another. I guess to feel that we each mattered—especially to each other.

"A great relationship," she added, "is—as I'm sure you know—a multitude of wondrous things."

She added, "I think at first that we loved each other more than we loved ourselves. I thought it was great. But that feeling didn't last long.

"Then the pain started. We didn't want to face it so we spent a lot of time just avoiding the issue by staying busy. I don't quite remember with what.

"Just when things looked as if they were going to come apart for us, life got better."

"What happened?" the nephew asked.

"Well, I didn't know. But something happened to Uncle. He downplayed it for a while. He said he'd just wised up. He was reluctant to tell me what the change was that had come over him."

"But you did find out, Auntie."

She smiled and said, "I did indeed! I more than found out what had happened to him. He did one simple thing that let so many of the other very important aspects of our relationship develop into more of what we each had hoped for.

"Then I learned," she added, "how to do the same myself. I suppose I should start at the beginning."

The nephew was pleased. He felt it was going to be a good long walk.

As he walked along, he asked his aunt something he'd been wanting to know for a long time.

"How," he asked, "can I get my basic needs met in a relationship?"

Auntie said, "You can get some very important needs met—like romance and tenderness and belonging. But you cannot get your primary needs met—like becoming happier. You must do that yourself.

"The minute any of us looks to a relationship to satisfy our own basic needs, we begin to experience pain. And we believe it's the other person's fault.

"I remember when your uncle and I tried very hard to take care of each other. But no matter what we did, it never seemed to be enough."

Then she smiled. "Now I feel well taken care of."

"How does Uncle take care of you now?"

"By first encouraging me to take very good care of myself. He also listens to me; brings me corny cards and flowers now and then; gives me support when I am upset; apologizes when he knows he's hurt me; plays with me and laughs with me . . . he does so many things he never used to do."

Auntie added, "Ever since he learned to take better care of himself, he's taken better care of us.

"In fact, of all the thoughtful things he does for me, the best is that he helps me take good care of myself."

The man was quiet. Then he asked, "How does Uncle help you do that?"

"He'll ask me questions like 'What are you going to do for yourself today, Honey?'

"He knows if I don't take better care of myself, sooner or later I'll find some reason to be annoyed with him—just because he's the one who is close at hand—even though I'm really annoyed with myself.

"And when I do take better care of myself, he knows I'll enjoy everything, including him, a good deal more.

"Uncle knows that our caring and communicating make our relationship work. He knows we need other people as well as ourselves to feel balanced and happy.

"So he'll say, 'I want you and me to be happy with you so take good care of you, Love. And let me know if I can help.'

"You see, he knows that because of the way I've been raised, I may not be willing to think of myself first. That's why he helps me do it.

"He seemed to give me permission in the beginning. Now I realize the gift he gave me. It was that I didn't need anyone's permission to take care of myself.

"I know now that it was and is for me. He just helps me see it. And, of course, he gets to enjoy the benefits as much as I do. So the more I do for myself, the more he likes it."

"Why is that?" the man wanted to know.

"Because when I take good care of myself," she answered with a burst of energy, "I feel truly alive and I'm a lot more fun to be around. And your uncle loves me that way."

"What do you do, Auntie, when he isn't paying any attention to you? When you feel unloved?"

"When I feel no one else is nurturing me, I feel unnurtured. So I nurture myself. I do some silly little thing for myself that makes me feel good— like getting an electric blanket, setting it to a comfortable level, and having it ready for me when I get into bed.

"Just the feeling of the electric blanket is nourishing and nurturing." She laughed and said, "I guess it's like being back in the warmth of the womb.

"Or you can use flannel sheets to get the same feeling of being nurtured and protected.

"The point is, I don't ask someone else to nurture me all the time. I do what I can myself.

"I also nurture myself by creating a beautiful environment because my environment affects me."

"Me too," her nephew said.

"I remember once I saw pictures of the Caribbean and just looking at them made me feel wonderful. So I used some of the same colors in our bedroom. I used the peach, beige, and blue colors of the sunset, the sand, and sky in a few pillows and throw rugs. It's just decorating but it really lifted our spirits.

"But I nurture myself most when I create a beautiful *internal* environment. In fact, there is one thing I finally learned from your uncle that has helped me enjoy my relationship with him more than anything.

"We are continually teaching each other this:

*

Even More Important
Than My Being Loved

Is My Being Loving

*

"I used to think," Auntie said, "that being loved was just about the most important thing in the world.

"That, however, was a time when I was unhappy."

"I don't understand," the man said. "I still think that being loved is most important."

Auntie leaned forward and asked, "Tell me. Have you ever really felt loved enough? By anyone?"

To give the man his privacy, his aunt did not wait for an answer.

"My wanting to be loved," she continued, "worse yet, my needing to be loved, had one very big drawback."

"What was that?"

"My wanting or needing to be loved depended totally upon someone outside myself.

"Before I knew better, I gave up taking care of myself. I simply asked someone else to do the job. And the irony was I wasn't taking care of myself in the most important area of my life—love!

"I was like most people. I wanted to be loved and I had a certain mental picture of how that should feel for me. Then I compared my picture against how well I thought the other person was loving me. I guess I unconsciously always gave them a grade."

The man smiled and said, "It's amazing how often they fail."

"*They* fail?" Auntie asked.

The man thought for a moment.

Auntie continued, "Whenever I used to focus on my need to be loved by someone else, I soon felt unloved."

The man had an instant insight.

He didn't know why he had never seen it before.

He said slowly as the realization came to him, "And when you felt unloved, you began to act unloving."

"Sure," Auntie said. "I used to get hurt because I felt I wasn't loved. So I would withdraw or get angry."

"And as you acted in an unloving manner," the man noted, "it became more difficult for someone to love you."

The more he thought about what he was hearing, the more the man began to see another way of looking at love. "Maybe," he said, "there is a better way to take care of myself."

Auntie laughed with the lightheartedness of someone who was happy.

"Now I spend less time trying to be loved by others," she said, "and more time loving others.

"I've learned so much about taking care of myself from your uncle that I can now help him take better care of himself. And we enjoy each other more."

"What do you do to help take care of Uncle?"

"Many things," Auntie answered. "For instance, sometimes when he is being too hard on himself, I remind him to care more for himself.

"I know that I feel best when I accept my self," she said. "And I encourage Uncle to do the same. I remind him that the more we each accept ourselves, the more we enjoy ourselves and each other."

"How does Uncle react to that?"

"Almost always he appreciates it because he soon starts to treat himself better. Then he feels better.

"Sometimes though, when he's not quite ready to get off his own back, he'll say, 'Maybe I can rent a saddle, strap it on my back, and be more comfortable!'

"Of course, as soon as we start laughing," she said, "or at least smiling, things get better—first for him and then for us."

The man liked what he felt in his aunt's presence. She felt so good about herself, she made him feel good too.

Then his mind challenged the idea once again.

"Don't tell me," the man began, "that there aren't times when what you want to do for yourself doesn't clash with what he wants."

He was surprised to hear the hostility in his voice and was a little embarrassed about speaking to his aunt this way. But he wanted to know.

"Of course," she said. "But that's true in any case. As Uncle says, 'The truth is, people are eventually going to do what they want to do anyway, so why kid ourselves.'

"If you give up and do what the other person wants against your own best interests, sooner or later you're going to become resentful. And then it is only a question of time before you, consciously or unconsciously, find a way to get back at the other person.

"I know it sounds terrible," Auntie said, "but it's the truth. When you bury your own self-interest in favor of someone else—especially if you're not aware of it—it festers and things usually get worse.

"So we avoid a larger problem later on by each of us taking care of ourselves now.

We do this by communicating and negotiating to help both of us get what we want."

"So," the man said, "the whole idea is first to feel good yourself—even if it doesn't totally please the other person at the moment. And then, as you feel happy and peaceful, go on to feel good about the other person."

"Yes," Auntie said. "And the important thing is, when you feel good about the other person, *show* it.

"It will be in their best interests. And that is what they are interested in.

"When Uncle encourages and supports me to take care of myself—I show him in a lot of ways how much I appreciate it."

The man wondered if it wasn't too good to be true. "But conflicts are bound to occur. What do you do?"

Auntie agreed. "It doesn't mean that there isn't going to be conflict. There is. But by honestly taking care of yourself, *as well as* the other person, you avoid larger conflicts with the other person later.

"Uncle and I have conflicts. We don't always like it when the other person is taking care of himself. Sometimes when we are feeling a little insecure, we feel as though we are being shut out.

"But in the middle of feeling insecure, we often go inside ourselves and quietly ask, 'Is there a better way right now for me to be taking care of Me?'

"When we do, we usually see that the other person is just doing what they need to do themselves and will come back to us feeling good—about themselves and about us.

"Uncle and I are happy together," Auntie said.

"We have each found a way to take wonderful care of ourselves. And I guess we really appreciate the other person's helping us to do so. And rewarding us when we do. We like who we are when we are with one another."

The man said, "That reminds me of Elizabeth Barrett Browning, the poet, who wrote: 'I love you. Not so much for what you are. As for what I am. When I am with you.'"

Auntie clapped her hands and said, "What more can I say?"

I T had been almost two months since the man had visited his aunt. He had already begun to put to use what he had learned.

"I'm glad to see you," Uncle said, as his favorite nephew entered his home again. "I understand you had a good walk and talk some time ago with Auntie."

"Yes," the man said. "She sure is a great lady!"

"I agree," Uncle said. "She's quite a woman. Did you learn anything from her? I know I always do."

The man said, "I've learned that she thinks you now have a great relationship with her."

"That's true," Uncle said. "But did she tell you it wasn't always that way?"

"Yes, she did. It has encouraged me to change what I was doing wrong with my wife and children and I must admit we are all getting along better.

"But," the man continued, "I'm not sure I understand. Why does each person's taking better care of himself or herself help our relationship? I've always thought that was kind of selfish and would cause problems."

Uncle said, "Let me explain with an example from your own life. You mentioned that since you spoke with Auntie you've begun to change what you do with your family. Can you tell me how you've changed?"

"Yes," the man answered. "Last night I came home tired from a rough day at the office." Both men smiled at the cliché. "Then something small almost ruined the evening."

"What happened?" Uncle wanted to know.

"I wanted to be greeted when I came home in a way that let me know that I was appreciated."

Uncle anticipated. "But you weren't."

"Well," the man said, "I sure didn't *feel* appreciated. My wife barely said hello.

"So I walked off alone. I felt bad. I must have been pretty tired to have reacted as I did, but as I played the scene over again in my mind, I'm afraid I just felt sorry for myself.

"Then," the man smiled, "I asked myself, 'Is there a better way for me to be reacting?'"

The man continued, "I realized that my wife didn't say it with much enthusiasm, but she did say 'Hello, *Dear.*' She didn't say 'Hello, Jerk.'"

Uncle laughed. "You heard the 'Dear.'"

"Yes. And that made me feel better. It turned out to be an enjoyable night at home."

"What did you do?"

"I remembered what Auntie had said: 'Even more important than my being loved is my being *loving.*'

"I just decided," the man said, "to take better care of myself by *loving* her instead of asking her to love me.

"I thought it would make me feel better. And it did. I went out and gave her a hug and told her I was happy to be home. I told her I loved her. She liked it! Then she said she was sorry she was so tired . . ."

"From a rough day," Uncle said with a smile.

"You got it," the man said. "She probably hadn't been taking very good care of herself either that day.

"I'm still amazed," the man added, "at how well this works. What a difference it makes to our happiness."

Uncle said, "The key to a good relationship is balance. And you just illustrated that.

"That means that we don't insist that the other person be thinking of us all the time," Uncle noted. "You showed that when you let go of your expectations of how you thought you should be greeted—and of your ego. And so you let go of your pain."

Uncle added, "I'm sure you can see how easily that incident last night could have turned into a blowup. That's what happens when one person, or worse, two people are not taking good care of themselves."

"So it works best," the man said, "when both people are taking better care of themselves and when each is helping the other take good care of himself or herself."

"Wonderful!" the older man exclaimed. "You are beginning to grasp one of the important ways of having a great relationship with another person."

The man said, "The key for me, then, is first having a great relationship with myself."

"Yes," Uncle said. "I remember when I didn't know this truth. It was a bad time in my life.

"I felt as if no one cared about me. Not even me. Nobody knew it, because I hid my feelings.

"I remember," the older man admitted. "I did something I had never done before and hope I'll never do again."

"What?" the man asked.

"At one point," Uncle said, "I came to believe that I was not *able* to love or to be loved.

"I used to stay in bed sometimes for days, telling myself that I was just tired. But when I look back now on those times, I realize that I was depressed. It wasn't okay for me to be depressed. I had always thought of myself as an optimistic person."

The man asked, "Why were you depressed?"

"That's the interesting thing. I had no reason to be depressed. Things were going well in my business. I had a nice house and family. I wasn't sick. I didn't have any problems. At least not any I could see. Slowly, over the years, I needed this time in bed more often—to rest, you understand."

Then Uncle added, "Actually, it was to get away."

"From what?" the man asked.

The older gentleman paused and the gleam went from his eye. "From myself," he admitted.

"It really wasn't *other* people's love that I needed. So, no matter how much love other people gave me, it was never enough. I never let it in."

"Then I saw a bumper sticker that read, 'Have You Hugged YOURSELF Today?' I realized I hadn't."

The man said, "I've seen the bumper sticker that says, 'Have You Hugged Your Kid Lately,' but never one that reads, 'Have You Hugged YOURSELF Today?'

"I'd like to get one of those stickers, or *two*," the man laughed, "and stick one on my *dashboard*."

Uncle laughed too. "After you hug yourself, you *want* to hug your kids."

"Before I could be loved by others," Uncle said, "I needed to be loved not by others but by me."

The man asked, "How did you learn to love yourself?"

"I tried," Uncle said, "but I couldn't love myself. So I learned to like myself. I had to start with small steps."

"Like getting out of bed?" the man asked.

Uncle smiled and said, "Yes, like getting out of bed. I remember lying there one day, tired, knowing darn well that I had had more rest than Rip Van Winkle.

"Then I simply asked myself, 'Is there a better way for me to act right now?'"

"Is that where this simple method came from?"

"Yes. It came when things got so bad even the 'old me' saw that I had gone off track."

Uncle noted, "I stop and ask myself that question rather often just so I never get so far off track again."

"So what did you do?"

"The ancient Chinese," Uncle answered, "said you can't pour fresh hot tea into a cup full of stale cold tea. Only when you stop doing what *doesn't* work, can things get better.

"So first, I stopped doing what didn't work. I got out of bed. Then, when I was tempted to 'rest,' I would ask myself if there wasn't a better way."

"You obviously found a better way," the nephew said. "What did you do for yourself?"

Uncle asked, "Do you remember what we talked about when you first came here?

"Well, nephew, that's what I did. I started to take better care of myself. I knew I had to or I would get myself in even more trouble.

"I began to do some things for myself that we talked about.

"When I consistently did something as simple as take One Minute for Myself, and I did this repeatedly, I then started making very different decisions for myself.

"As I took as good care of myself as I did of other parts of my life, things started to get better for me. Then they got better between your aunt and me."

The man still found it hard to believe.

Uncle sensed his doubt and asked, "Imagine how you would feel if you asked someone you loved to hug you. In your mind, feel them hugging you. Now, how does that feel?"

"Good," the man said. "It feels good."

Uncle responded, "Sure. It's great to be hugged once in a while. Now imagine the person refuses to hug you."

The man looked surprised. He imagined how he would feel. "Rejected," he said, "and hurt." Then he added, "Angry." He paused and said quietly, "Sometimes it feels like that at home."

"Sure. Who do you really need to hug you?"

The man was silent. "Myself," he said quietly.

"Of course," Uncle said. "That is why we feel so much better when we stop and are quiet and listen to our Best Self—that part of us that knows what we need.

"Getting in touch with our Best Self," Uncle said, "is like giving ourselves a perfect hug."

Then Uncle asked the man, "When you haven't hugged yourself enough, can anyone hug you often enough, or warm enough, or . . . ?"

The man began to see what his uncle had been talking about: "We can never, never get enough of what we don't need."

"When I do not take care of myself," the man realized, "I do not get my own basic needs met. I then ask others to do for me what only I can do. And they never do it enough.

"Because others cannot meet my needs," the man saw, "I have trouble in my relationships with other people."

Uncle said, "You are learning well."

"Do you wonder," Uncle asked, "why such an approach doesn't work?"

"So I can't have a wonderful relationship with anyone else," the nephew said, "until I have one with me."

"Can you say that in a more positive way?"

The man smiled. "The most important relationship I will ever have is the one I have now with myself."

"Great. Now what do you think is true in a relationship with two people?"

"Now that I think of it," his nephew said, "I can't have a great relationship with anyone else until I have a good one with me and they have a good one with themselves."

Uncle asked, "How could you present that idea so you and your loved ones could all learn the lesson?"

The man thought and then said:

*

We Can Have A Wonderful
Relationship Together

When I Have One With Me
And You Have One With You

*

"Now you've got it!"

Then Uncle cautioned, "But will you make a commitment to yourself and your family?

"I recall," Uncle said, "when Auntie asked me to make a commitment to *my* family. We were having a rough time. And I wasn't sure I wanted to make it.

"She asked for a commitment from me not just for faithfulness in marriage but for something much more."

"What did she ask you to commit to?"

Uncle answered, "She asked me not to run away—not to leave or ask her to leave because of any one incident—however upset or fearful I might be.

"In short, she asked me to make a commitment not to run away from *myself*."

Uncle continued, "If I agreed, she said, she wouldn't run from herself. Or if she did run—even if it was just in her own mind—she would get right back to being with herself and with us as soon as she could."

"So the commitment really was that you each promised to take good care of *yourself*," the man realized. "And one good way of doing that was not to run away from yourself."

Uncle smiled and said, "I think your wife's going to be happy you're coming home tonight."

Uncle said, "I have enjoyed your visits over the last few months. Talking with you let me realize how different my life is now from the time I was so unhappy."

Uncle added, "It's strange to remember that there was a time when it wasn't this way."

His uncle looked happy and at peace with himself.

The man was very encouraged. He knew that his life might be as good one day.

In fact, it had already begun. He just needed to put his doubts aside long enough to *do* what he was discovering really worked for him and his family.

"Come back in a while if you like," Uncle suggested.

"Let me know if things continue to improve in your family when you all begin to help one another take care of yourselves.

"If so, there is something more important you and your family and neighbors may want to know."

When Uncle left the room, the man made a few summary notes of what he felt was important.

Then he went out into the backyard to say thank-you to his aunt and uncle.

:01 *Taking Care of We: A Summary*

It helps me have a better relationship with other people when I remember:

- When we've taken good care of ourselves, we can share our Best Selves with each other.

- When we nurture ourselves, we can then go on to better nurture one another.

- More important than my being loved is my being loving.

- We may have some small conflict now, but we avoid much larger and more serious conflicts later, when each of us takes better care of ourselves.

- Our commitment is not to run away from ourselves, but for each of us to take good care of ourselves and to take good care of one another.

- We can help ourselves and each other by asking, "Have You Hugged YOURSELF Today?"

- We can have a wonderful relationship together, when I have one with me, and you have one with you.

PART IV

The World Benefits

T HE man had been told that if he wanted to know something very important, he should return to his uncle. He had. It had been quite a journey for him over the last three months and he'd learned a great deal.

As he was welcomed into the older man's study, he saw shelves of books and a globe in the corner.

The man remembered that first conversation when his uncle had spun the globe and had said that the other people—ones who benefited as much as we did by our taking care of ourselves— might be members of his family or strangers on the other side of the world.

"I'm beginning to see," the man said, "that taking care of yourself can lead to peace."

His uncle smiled. "How did you discover that?"

"Because," the man responded, "I've learned that when I take good care of myself, I am not angry. I am peaceful. I now see that peace is both the absence of anger and the presence of love— especially toward myself."

The man added, "My wife and children have noticed a big improvement in my peacefulness.

"And when they saw the effect taking care of myself had on me, they asked me to help them learn how to take better care of themselves. Now we find each other more enjoyable to be with.

"Our family is happier," the man said.

"You *seem* happier," Uncle noted. "Now you may be able to understand this:

*

When Every Person In The World
Takes Better Care Of Themselves,

Everyone In The World Will Feel
Better Taken Care Of

And Then We May Finally
Begin To Care More
About Each Other

*

"It is not just idealistic," Uncle said. "It is practical—as it has been for you and your family."

The doubtful man asked, "What can a person in poverty and injustice do in only one minute?"

"Because I am not him, I cannot know," Uncle answered. "But if he really stops, looks, and listens to the best part of himself, he will discover it for himself."

Knowing his nephew had the answer within him, Uncle asked, "When is it more important for us to take good care of ourselves—when things are going well or poorly for us?"

"When things are going poorly," the man answered. "There may be no one to help us, so we need to nurture ourselves."

Uncle agreed. "What usually makes you happiest—doing big or little things for yourself?"

The man answered, "To my constant surprise, it's the little things—like changing my attitude."

"I agree," Uncle noted. "It may be almost impossible to change the terrible conditions outside. But each of us can change conditions inside ourselves."

Uncle asked, "Why wouldn't every person who took better care of himself, by doing the little things for himself—regardless of his situation— be less angry with himself and more peaceful? Wouldn't a person who is less angry be more apt to take better care of others?

"Why then," Uncle asked, "wouldn't the world be a better place if we—particularly those of us in difficulty—each nurtured ourselves more?"

The man thought about it.

"So you're saying that it is not going to solve all the problems of the world," the man realized. "But if all people took *better* care of themselves, however they chose to do it, the world would be a *better* place. People would be *less* angry."

Uncle said, "Yes. It isn't absolute but all of us are better served when each of us takes *better* care of ourselves. When we do, we want to cooperate. Cooperate means 'Co-operate.' I operate me; and you operate you. It is the ultimate in freedom and responsibility.

"When people assume this responsibility of taking better care of themselves, they are not as dependent on unreliable organizations.

Uncle cautioned, "We need to balance helping people who temporarily need our help, with helping them discover how to take better care of themselves.

"A group of people, in fact, want to erect a statue on the western side of the United States to balance the Statue of Liberty.

"'The Statue of Response Ability' would be dedicated to the ability each of us has to respond to what is the best in us—in order to ensure our personal liberty."

The young man's face lit up. "I had always thought of responsibility as something I didn't really want to do but was supposed to do. Now I see it is really an ability I have to respond to my world. I like that.

"I now also see the obvious," the man realized. The man spoke slowly. "Peace begins with me."

ALONE in his own home, many months later, the man reflected on all he had learned to do.

While he thought it would be wonderful if the whole world improved, he had accepted the immediate challenge of improving his *own* world.

He had found a way to discover inner success: to simply stop, look and listen to his Best Self. And he did it every day. He was learning.

In fact, he had learned the most important lesson of his entire life: inner success is *loving* yourself.

Eventually this lead to his greater outer success.

He had worried in the beginning that taking care of himself was self-centered. He now realized that it was his *not* taking care of himself that was selfish. Because that caused many problems for himself and other people.

He had discovered the tranquility of taking care, with equal consideration, of Me, Thee, and We.

To this, the man added his own vision.

He had come to see life as more attractive not just because he had learned how to be a caretaker, as Uncle had suggested. But because he had also learned how to be a care *giver*.

The more easily he gave to himself, the more he gave to others. He once thought giving was better than receiving and so he had always had trouble receiving. Perhaps he had been more comfortable giving because when he was receiving, he was not in control. Now he balanced giving and receiving.

He saw that if no one receives, no one can give.

And so he learned to *give* to himself and to *receive* from himself. He felt the peace within him.

The man discovered the wisdom of what others had known down through the ages: *The answer lies within me.*

He liked his uncle's concept of the Best Self. And he would always use it to find his happiness.

However, the man had developed another name for it. He liked to think of that quiet, wise part of him as "The Intuitive." He realized that when he listened to the intuitive part of himself, he made better decisions.

He knew that the word "Intuitive" began with the letter "I." He thought, *"'I,'"* like other people, can find the answers when I listen to that intuitive part of myself—my 'best' self."

He saw it had nothing to do with his ego. He thought, "When I lose my ego, I gain my self."

The man knew that it was only when he let go of his egotistical, controlling self that he finally made contact with a greater power. Perhaps it was the same power that many people called "God"— the God that was within him—the part of him that was wiser than he usually was, and far greater than himself. Whatever name a person called it, the man knew he had found a reliable source of quiet power.

The One Minute he often gave himself to stop, look, and listen, quietly led him to the best part of him. He knew he would go on to discover more.

It was only the beginning.

Then the man heard a car enter his driveway. His wife and children were home. He was happy, he liked seeing them. He had given his family a great gift—the gift of his Best Self. He and his family were obviously happier.

So, too, were many people he worked with.

As he went to greet his family, he remembered the men and women who had shared their personal secrets with him: Uncle's business associate; her husband, the artist; Auntie; and, of course, Uncle, himself.

They had each taught him to balance his life by both giving to *and* receiving from himself.

He was happy that he had taken so many notes. He could share what was written down with others.

It wasn't so much that he had learned anything new. In fact, most of what he had discovered was a confirmation of what he somehow already knew.

What *was* new was that he had found a practical way in a busy world to *use* what he knew worked.

He stopped, looked and listened.

He often *stopped* for One Minute. He *looked* at what he was thinking and doing. He asked himself, "What is the best way to take good care of myself?"

Then he *listened quietly to himself for an answer* which inevitably came to him from his Best Self— that part of him that knew what was best for him.

When he *clearly* saw what was best, he usually did it. As a way of thanking the people who had helped him learn, he decided to share the information with the people around him. He realized:

*

It's Just Good Business,

*For You To Take That
Important One Minute
For Your "Self"*

*And To Encourage Others
To Do The Same.*

*

the end

Spencer Johnson, M.D., is an internationally bestselling author whose books help millions of people discover simple truths they can use to have healthier lives with more success and less stress.

He is the originator and coauthor of *The One Minute Manager*®, the #1 *New York Times* bestseller, written with legendary management consultant Kenneth Blanchard, Ph.D. The book continues to appear on business bestseller lists and has become the most popular management method in the world.

Dr. Johnson has written many bestsellers, including five other books in the *One Minute*® series: *The One Minute $ales Person*, *The One Minute Mother*™, *The One Minute Father*™, *One Minute for Yourself*™, and *The One Minute Teacher*™; *Yes or No;* the popular *ValueTales*™ children's books; and the perennial gift favorite, *The Precious Present*.

His education includes a B.A. in psychology from the University of Southern California, an M.D. degree from the Royal College of Surgeons, and medical clerkships at Harvard Medical School and The Mayo Clinic.

Dr. Johnson was medical director of communications for Medtronic, the inventors of cardiac pacemakers; research physician at The Institute for Inter-Disciplinary Studies, a think tank; and consultant to the Center for the Study of the Person, and to the School of Medicine, University of California.

His books have been featured often in the media, including CNN, *Today, Larry King Live, Time* magazine, *USA Today, The Wall Street Journal*, and United Press International.

There are more than eleven million copies of Spencer Johnson's books in print in twenty-six languages.